1 MONTH OF
FREE
READING

at

www.ForgottenBooks.com

By purchasing this book you are eligible for one month membership to ForgottenBooks.com, giving you unlimited access to our entire collection of over 1,000,000 titles via our web site and mobile apps.

To claim your free month visit:

www.forgottenbooks.com/free1018782

ISBN 978-0-331-14254-9
PIBN 11018782

This book is a reproduction of an important historical work. Forgotten Books uses state-of-the-art technology to digitally reconstruct the work, preserving the original format whilst repairing imperfections present in the aged copy. In rare cases, an imperfection in the original, such as a blemish or missing page, may be replicated in our edition. We do, however, repair the vast majority of imperfections successfully; any imperfections that remain are intentionally left to preserve the state of such historical works.

THE MILITARY BAND

A Resume of the History of Military Music

Ever since our hairy naked forefather stepped to the door of his cave and lifted the hollowed out thigh bone to his lips and blew a blast which roused the surrounding members of his tribe to the fighting mood, music in some form has been a part of all armies; a stimulant on the march; a re-enforcement in the fight; and a lullaby at night when the day's fight and toil were past. The sound of the trumpet has waked the world to toil, called it to fight and pray, and mourned over the last resting place when all work was over. Without music, no function was considered complete. Half of the mystery of the various religions which the world has known has been enhanced by low hidden music. The soothing strains of music have soothed the turbulent spirit of fighting kings; quieted the ferociousness of wild beasts; and charmed the serpent from his lair.

The tuck of drum and the skirl of fife have always been war's alarum and have stirred the hearts of men to warlike action since the earliest times. What boy has not hurried toward their sound, and how many have followed them to death or victory? After the long march when spirits are fagged and muscles aching, the music of the band has put new heart into man; and when the fight is over and the victory is won, all strife, danger and disaster are forgotten in a paen of victory.

Military music has a strange history and the development to its present high standard has been slow and by degrees. The trumpet, fife and drum have ever been the predominant instruments, the ancient predecessors of these being the tambour and fife, tambour and trumpet and the hand drum. The Egyptians used the tambour, trumpet and harp for their military music; the ancient Assyrians and the Persians, the tambour, fife and trumpet. Greek military music consisted of trumpets, hand drums, and fifes. The Romans used the trumpet, drum and the predecessor of our present oboe, a primitive hautbois.

The African savage was stirred to war-like valor by the beating of drums made of wood and hide, beaten by the hand. In Moro land the war music consisted of brass tom-toms of various sizes, sometimes arranged in octaves and which really were musical.

Medieval times brought the minstrel and the minstrel Knight with his "Band" of players who wandered from castle to castle playing martial and other music. The minstrel played the harp and roused his hearers to valorous deeds by recommitting tales of local heroes. The long Saga of the Norseman with its wondrous tales of the deeds of long dead kings and leaders, stirred the hearers to boldness and desire to emulate the men of old.

Before the days of writing on paper and the compilation of written history, the records of peoples and countries were preserved by means of the song of the Skalds, Minstrels and story-tellers. These living histories recount the lives of kings, the stories of their combats and conquests and keep the memory of the people alive to the history of their country.

The first military band as such seems to have been one formed by Henry VIII King of England about 1560, which formed for his regiment of guards, commonly known as the Beef Eaters. The band was composed of trombones, viols, rebecs, bagpipes and drums. Discription of the music rendered is not made, but is said to have been "beauteous."

Louis XIV of France had a band formed of hautbois, trombones, viols, cymbals, and drums. While this was formed as a band it was not distinctly a military band.

There seems to have been a gradual

(Continued on page 19)

HEADQUARTERS U. S. ARMY BASE HOSPITAL
Camp Grant, Illinois

June 21, 1919.

A letter to the Band.

All of us hate for our friends to leave us, and in military circles it is discouraging to have a highly efficient element of one's organization permanently separated. The discharge of our band is applicable to the above conditions.

Through the able organization and administration of the band, this organization has been the pride of the hospital, and has entertained the personnel and thousands of patients. It has participated in every large patriotic drive, and has visited almost every city in the state of Illinois for the good of others. These visits have been followed by numerous letters of praise for your conduct, efficiency and military appearance. There has not been a letter of any other form of criticism.

It is with great pleasure that I am able to say that during your existence of fourteen months, there has not been a court martial or even so simple a punishment as company punishment in your ranks. This shows that you have performed your duty properly, and is a manifestation of the highest military attainment. Your director, Hospital Sergeant Henry P. VorKeller, Medical Department, is a soldier, an organizer and an administrator. Your ranks are composed of gentlemen and musicians who have performed their duties in the proper manner. You have done your bit. May you return to your homes and business knowing that your Commanding Officer is well pleased with your work, and the entire Base Hospital will miss you.

N. C. Michie,
Lieut. Colonel, Medical Corps, U. S. A.,
Commanding.

BASE HOSPITAL BAND
CAMP GRANT...NOV. 24TH '18

THE SILVER CHEV'

Official Publication of the U. S. Army Base Hospital, Camp Grant, Illinois.
Published by Authority of the Surgeon-General of the U. S. Army.

Editor
SGT. JOHN H. NELSON

Business Manager
SGT. 1st Cl. H. O. BARNVILLE

Departments
HOSP. SGT. HOWARD M. GOODSPEED

Photography
SGT. 1st CL. SAMUEL A. SHOUP

Contributing Staff

WILLIAM H. KIRCHNER..Detachment News
RALPH S. DEWEY...Athletic News
H. R. SWEET...Band News
CAPTAIN GEORGE S. DUNTLEY, M. C...................................Photography
1ST LIEUT. CARL E. WISMER, S. C..........Welfare Activities, Recreational Activities
CAPTAIN W. W. BAUER, M. C.................................Officers' News, Advisor

Good-Bye and Good Luck

A large number of the men of this Detachment are prone to think of the members of the Band as leading the life of the mythical Riley; that their work has been less necessary to the prosecution of the war than that of many others. Unfortunately we cannot treat these gentlemen to the exquisite pleasure of marching along a dusty street blowing a tuba for an hour; or the equally delightful and restful occupation of playing from eight until ten thirty at a dance, while the mercury is making a vain attempt to force its way through the top of the thermometer, and their special girl floats demurely by in the arms of another. And as for accomplishing results, a perusal of the history of the Band, appearing on another page, may lead some to change their opinion in regard to both the amount and the value of the work done by this organization.

The Detachment as a whole will miss the Band. Retreat will never be the same ceremonious function without it, and those who enjoy dancing will especially regret the departure of the "Jazz Hounds" who have furnished such delightful music at our social functions.

The Leisure Hours

Recreation and the proper employment of the leisure hours is just as essential to success as application during working hours. The large majority of people are of the impression that when they have struggled through the hours they are "assigned to duty" that it really makes very little difference how the remaining hours are spent. Nothing could be farther from the truth. The interest you will be able to take in your work, the pleasure you may get out of it depends largely upon the way your leisure hours are spent. The man in perfect physical health, who spends his hours off duty in a wholehearted enjoyment of such recreation as is offered him is seldom found nursing a grouch.

Although a number of us have in a sense missed out on the "healthy outdoor life of the American Army" by being assigned to duty in the medical corps, the man who does not return to civil life with a strong healthy physique is not taking advantage of the opportunities offered him. Why not get out and play a few games of tennis or volley ball these long light evenings, so that when you return to civil life you will be able to take a new grip on the rungs of the ladder of life.

F CLEF JOTTINGS

Speaking of the League of Nations —have you heard of the League of Privates? The ten privates of the band, recently organized, have at last succeeded in getting a sufficient amount of work out of the seventeen non-coms under them.

Oh! The Non-Coms get the clover,
But the Privates put it over,
And the privates are getting back.

Were Sgt. Zurawski spending his furloughs and passes at Delavan, WISCONSIN, we could blame it on the lake, but WHAT can it be that takes him to Delavan, ILLINOIS?

The band's stage-song popularity contest has just ended in a whirlwind finish. "Illinois" and "On Wisconsin" ran neck and neck for several days, but "Illinois" nosed in at the finish with a vote of twelve to its opponent's eleven, due to the last minute loyalty of Pvt. Prather to his wife's state. "Iowa" and "All Hail Minnesota" were hopelessly out of the running, securing three and one votes, respectively. "Illinois" might have secured "All Hail Minnesota's" vote, by using a little diplomacy and reminding Pvt. Korfhage that Springfield is in Illinois.

Imagine yourself a few months hence, in civies, wandering lonesomely about in a strange city, some thousand miles from home and friends, (at least you think so) when, lo, you are arrested by a familiar sound. You halt, uncertainly, unable to believe your ears. Yes, there it is again: this time

a little louder and shriller. You whistle a response, turn quickly and see, rushing across the street to join you, "Sti," "Bab," "The Pog," Sherrick or anyone of the boys of the old "Base" band and you know that your loneliness, for that evening at least, is banished. Oh, boy! Ain't it a grand and glorious feeling? Little as that strain may mean to the lay-man, to the man who has played in the Base Hospital Band, it will stand for good fellowship and comradeship, and wherever the members meet, till parched and wrinkled lips will no more respond to the promptings of a thrilled brain, its stirring notes will be joyfully exchanged.

"Red Pepper Burns," so does gasoline, as one of the boys discovered on the tour, when he did a hurry up job of cleaning his leggings, got his ankles soaked and then paraded on a hot day. S. O. S. for "Dock" Stucki.

What would have happened to the band without Corp. (Doc) John C. Stucki is to be shuddered at and left to the most horrible imaginings. In the barracks or on tour, he has been doctor, lawyer, adviser and general emergency repair man. If he hasn't it in his grip, it's in one of his capacious pockets—be the need for a "C C" pill, monkey wrench, piccolo-pad, earmuff, hair-spring for a watch or a Ford carburetor. Three Rahs for Stucki!!!

The Pullman Co. has had to recarpet the "Gibraltar" since the Victory Loan tour, on account of the path worn to "Doc" Stucki's berth by the members of the party.

The latest in refined music—Pvt. Riha putting "the Streets of Cairo" break into "Does She? I'll Say She Does" on his Eb clarinet.

We were about to mention the volley-ball tournament, but—let's talk about pleasant subjects.

(Continued on page 20)

Votava   Ruedebusch   Babbitt

Korthage   Riha   Garling

Wohlfahrt   Prather   Sweet

THE BAND HISTORY

Having felt for some time, the need, in the Base Hospital, of a musical organization of its own, Lieut. Col. Michie, collaborating with Maj. Baum and Maj. Clark, in April, 1918, organized the Base Hospital Band.

The beginning was a very modest one, the first members being drawn entirely from the Medical Detachment. Several of the men had had previous musical experience, but most of the charter members started in to learn instruments they had never played before.

After a study of the needs of the band, instruments were purchased and issued to the men, under the supervision of the late Sgt. Horton.

The embryo band-men continued at their regular hospital duties, taking an hour or so off in the forenoon for rehearsal and in the afternoon for individual practice in the woods, near the river, where their discords would be least distracting to the rest of the personnel.

Sgt. Colles, director of the 342nd Infantry Band, who later earned a commission and went to France with his organization, was secured to come daily, with a few of his best men, to coach and instruct the members at the rehearsals in the Y. M. C. A. chapel.

It soon became apparent, that if a band of the desired quality were to be attained, outside talent would be necessary. By "scouting," a number of high grade men were discovered and transferred to the Detachment from the Depot Brigade and other organizations. Among these, was Pvt. Henry P. Vorkeller, who stood out pre-eminent among the other men by reason of his knowledge of and execution upon the saxophone and cornet. Sgt. Colles immediately made him assistant director and shortly afterward, placed him in full charge.

At that time, a reorganization took place and the men who had made the least progress were replaced by men of more experience. This done, results

were rapidly secured and the band was able to take its proper place in the activities of the hospital.

The first public appearance was at noon on Decoration Day, May 30th, 1918, at the hospital flag-raising, and a few days later found the band playing regularly at retreat.

At that time also, was organized, from the personnel of the band, the Base Hospital Orchestra, which has expanded and made a name for itself, not only in Camp, but in many cities within a radius of a hundred miles.

On Saturday, June 15th, 1918, the band, together with a number of nurses from the hospital, participated in the big Red Cross parade in Chicago, making a very creditable showing, considering its youth.

Pvt. Vorkeller's leadership having been approved by Col. Michie, he was given the rank of Corporal, from which he has since risen to that of Hospital Sergeant. His wide acquaintance among musicians in Chicago and elsewhere enabled him to secure the induction into the band of a number of high grade band and orchestra men, among them, Sgt. 1st/Cl Zurawski, cornetist; Sgt. 1st/Cl Verhoeff, drummer; Sgt. Votava, pianist and drummer; Pvt. Sam Haase, violinist; Pvt. Wumkes, saxophonist; and Pvt. 1st/Cl Bodenschatz, drummer.

The addition of these men, together with a number of others, recruited from other sources, put the band on a musical plane where it has been a credit, not only to its founders, but to the institution it represents.

Once known, the demand for the services of the band, from camp and from the country at large has been constant. Lieut.-Col. Michie has not been selfish in this matter and has allowed the people of southern Wisconsin and practically all of Illinois to share with the Base Hospital in the enjoyment of its music.

The functions of the band have been

many in the fifeen months of its existence. Under its influence, the Base Hospital "Retreat" became one of the most impressive military rites in camp. Not only has music been furnished for the Detachment and Officers' drill and review, but the band, during the period of the war, frequently participated in "guard-mount," reviews and parades for the C. O. T. S. and other camp organizations.

In their capacity as morale lifters, the band and orchestra have furnished concerts and music for dances, picnics, parties, athletic contests and barbecues for the enlisted men, officers, nurses and convalescents. At six o'clock on Christmas morning carols were played in the corridors of the hospital by the band, and throughout the day and evening the orchestra was kept busy, trying to make the day as pleasant as possible for those who had to stay over in camp.

Such an orchestra, made up as it has been, of some of the leading hotel and cabaret musicians of Chicago and other cities, will probably never again be available for dances in this locality, and lucky has been the dance management that has been able to secure the services of Sgt. Vorkeller's men.

During the fall, the band furnished music at several "community sings" at Rockford, the Horse Show at Seward, a community concert at Aurora and County Fairs at Belvidere and Warren, Ill. Hospital Units 58, 20 and 37 were proudly escorted to the depot, when they entrained for overseas, as were also several units of the 86th Division.

Commencing September 21st, four hard but successful weeks' work were put in helping put Chicago "over the top" in the Fourth Liberty Loan. While on this drive, the band boys were so fortunate as to escape the "flu" epidemic, which took so large a toll from the camp and hospital personnel.

Three weeks later saw the boys again in Chicago, working on the United War Activities drive. This was carried to a successful conclusion after ten days' work. Again, in December, ten days were devoted to the Red Cross Membership Drive in Chicago.

The biggest task tackled and carried through successfully, was that of helping the state of Illinois raise its quota in the Victory Liberty Loan. Five weeks were devoted to this, a tour being made on a special war trophy exhibit train. Previous to the tour, which took three weeks, a week of parading and concert work was put in at Chicago and at the termination, another hard week was spent on the streets of that city.

During the demobilization period, this past winter, twice weekly, the band took its turn at putting pep into the discharge meetings held daily at the Liberty Theatre.

Not always has its work been that of cheer, for on five occasions it has been called on to serve at military funerals.

At its prime, the band consisted of thirty-five men, but from time to time, especially meritorious cases have been discharged, until, at present, the band muster-roll calls for twenty-seven men and "Spot," the coach-dog mascot, who, since his adoption, early on the Victory Loan tour, has had his place in the ranks of the band and affection of the members.

Soon after the organization of the band, its members were taken from their various duties and made answerable entirely to their director, Sgt. Vorkeller. Separate barracks were furnished them and, for the past fifteen months, they have lived together as one big family, establishing friendships that will endure for a lifetime.

Unable, itself, to win glory overseas, the Base Hospital Band has done what it could, in its small way, toward making life more bearable for the others, who, like themselves, have had to "fight" over here without the tonic of excitement to carry them on, and for those, who, having fought "over there," have been invalided back to recuperate before going home.

Now that the big need is over, the members are glad of the opportunity

(Continued on page 23)

BAND NEWS

At last, seeing the unevenness of the contest, Miss Olson joined forces with the band and by her efficient work on first base, saved the team from total demoralization. Corp. Stucki proved himself more than a hero by wading bravely into the turbulent depths of the Kishwaukee and rescuing the ball, which had gotten far beyond its depth and was about to sink for the third and last time.

All this occurred at the picnic given by Lieut. Col. Michie, as a farewell to the Bluebirds, in a pretty little grove on the banks of the Kishwaukee, near Cherry Valley. Needless to say, a grand and glorious time was enjoyed by all. After the strenuous ball game, no second call for supper had to be sounded. You should have seen that bunch eat. The commissary Ford came back to camp a whole lot lighter than when it went out.

After "chow," the band got together and tried to reciprocate in some measure, for the good time shown them. Here, again, Miss Olson showed her versatility by "directing" the band in a very dramatic rendition of the "Tenth Regiment" march. True, she had to call on her trusty corpsmates to help round up the boys who had forgotten that "in union there is strength"

and had taken solo positions thither and anon.

Taken as a whole, Wednesday, May 18th, will go in the band diary (and possibly in that of the Bluebirds) as SOME day.

One Bluebird remarked on the beauty of Corp. Muehlbrandt's flaxen hair. "Yes," said another, "it's too bad he isn't a dog."

On July second, the band boys are planning on holding a farewell dinner in the "Rainbow Room" at Waltzingers' in Rockford. It is expected that most of the boys who formerly belonged to the organization, but are now enjoying civilian bliss, will be present. A splendid menu has been prepared and with a snappy program of toasts, a never-to-be-forgotten evening will undoubtedly be spent. Following the dinner, a theatre party will be given at the Palace. Pretty souvenir program-menus have been secured for the occasion. It is the plan of the band boys to form an association and hold annual banquets, whereby the goodfellowship of the organization may be perpetuated.

(Continued on page 23)

BASEBALL

BASE HOSPITAL VS. CAMP DODGE

Camp Dodge, June 17, 1919.

In a game replete with much spectacular fielding the Camp Grant team took the Dodge team into camp to the tune of 2-1. The Grant team played air-tight ball throughout and brought the athletic carnival held at Camp Dodge on that date to an adverse termination for the home contingent.

Houck's steady pitching featured the game, retiring the side in the seventh inning on four pitched balls. Dodge started the scoring in the fourth. Roach singled and went to second on a balk. Higgins fanned and Roache stole third. Coughlin singled, but was out trying to make it into a double, Crabtree to Saubert, but Roache had scored. Meyers singled and stole second. Palmer fanned.

The Grant team came back in the sixth to tie the count. Crabtree flied to Roache. Martin dropped Houck's pop-up. H. Johnson walked. Meyers allowed Martin's throw to get past him and Houck scored, and H. Johnson going to third. P. Johnson and Glumske both fanned. The Grant team won the game in the eighth inning. Houck fanned. Meyers fumbled H. Johnson's grounder and Johnson stole second. P. Johnson fanned. Glumske doubled along the left field foul line scoring

H. Johnson, which proved to be the winning run.

The Dodge team made a valiant attempt to tie the count in the last half of the ninth. Donahue singled. Larler, batting for Roache, flied to Glumske. Glumske attempted to catch Donahue sleeping off first base, but threw wild and Donahue reached third. Houck then fanned Higgins and caught Donahue at home trying to steal.

The Grant team greatly appreciated the splendid treatment accorded them in their stay at Dodge.

This was the hardest game on the trip and every man on the team was on the job from start to finish. Glumske had badly sprained his ankle at Snelling, but being the only catcher available, gamely stuck to his post and put up a fine game in spite of that fact.

Box Score for Camp Dodge game:

Camp Grant.

	AB	R	H	PO	A	E
H. Johnson, 3b	3	1	0	2	1	0
P. Johnson, C.F.	4	0	1	1	0	0
Glumske, C.	4	0	1	9	2	1
Saubert, S.S.	4	0	0	1	1	0
Guiger, L.F.	4	0	1	4	0	0
Kawa, 2b	4	0	0	1	2	0
Truso, R.F.	4	0	1	1	0	0
Crabtree, 1b	4	0	0	8	0	0
Houck, P.	3	1	0	0	2	0
Totals	34	2	4	27	8	1

Camp Dodge.

	AB	R	H	PO	A	E
Ryan, 2b 4	4	0	0	1	3	0
Donahue, 3b 4	4	0	1	2	2	1
Roache, C. 3	3	1	2	10	0	0
Higgins, C.F. 4	4	0	0	2	0	0
Coughlin, R.F. 4	4	0	1	0	0	0
Meyers, 1b 3	3	0	1	12	1	2
Palmer, L.F........3	3	0	0	0	0	0
Hartzell, S.S. 2	2	0	0	0	1	0
Martin, P..........3	3	0	0	0	4	2
*Lally 1	1	0	0	0	0	0
Totals 31	31	1	5	27	11	5

*Batted for Roache in 9th.

Summary—Two base hit: Glumske. Struck out: by Houck 7, by Martin 7. Base on balls: off Houck 1, off Martin 1. Balk: Houck. Stolen bases: Roache, Meyers, Hartzell, H. Johnson.

BASE HOSPITAL VS. FT. SNELLING

Ft. Snelling, Minn., June 14, 1919. The baseball team started their six day trip to Ft. Snelling, Camp Dodge and Ft. Des Moines inauspiciously, but by no means ignominiously, by going down to defeat before the strong Ft. Snelling team. The feature of the game was the very ragged work of the umpires, both Snelling men. The decisions rendered against the Camp team necessitated our men walking off the field on three or four separate occasions. It was just the true sportsmanship of our men (which was an exact antithesis to the spirit of the Snelling crowd) that made our men complete the game. We've our chance coming for a return game with Snelling is booked for June 25 on our field and our boys are out for a slaughter in retaliation.

Crabtree's pitching and fielding featured the fray and with more perfect support behind him by his mates, our boys would have carried home the bacon in spite of the adverse conditions under which they had to struggle, for every one of Snelling's runs were unearned.

The Grant team was the first to counter, getting one score in the initial frame. Wigdor, who was crippled and incapacitated during the trip, was sent in to bat for H. Johnson and singled to second after P. Johnson had fanned. Houck ran for Wigdor and stole second, advancing to third on an overthrow to second. He scored a moment later on a wild pitch.

Ft. Snelling tied the score in the fourth after two were out. Nelson fumbled Schultz's grounder and he went to second and then stole third. McCann was hit and Schultz and McCann pulled a double steal, the former scoring.

Our men forged ahead in the fifth. Kawa doubled and stole third. Truso walked. Nelson fanned. Crabtree and Kawa then engineered a perfect squeeze play, Kawa scoring and Crabtree making first, Truso landing on third. P. Johnson fanned and H. Johnson walked, filling the bases. Glumske lost the golden opportunity by fanning.

Snelling came right back in their end of the fifth and tied the count. Vaughn bunted out to Crabtree. Lushen singled and reached third on a single by Brown. Tew hit to Saubert, who fumbled and allowed Lushen to score and Brown to reach third. Porter and Anderson flied out to Guiger and Kawa respectively.

With the score tied, the game was nip-and-tuck until Snelling came to bat in the ninth. Brown, the first man up, doubled to left-center and P. Johnson's speedy return to Saubert should have nailed the batter as he tried to stretch the hit into a triple, but Saubert heaved the ball over third base into the stands and allowed the winning run to counter. The box score:

Grant.

	AB	R	H	PO	A	E
P. Johnson, C.F.....5	5	0	0	3	0	1
H. Johnson, 3b.....2	2	0	0	1	0	0
Glumske, C. 4	4	0	0	7	0	0
Saubert, S.S. 4	4	0	1	0	1	3
Guiger, L.F. 3	3	0	0	1	0	0
Kawa, 2b 4	4	1	1	2	1	0
Truso, R.F.........3	3	0	2	0	0	0
Nelson, 1b 4	4	0	0	8	0	1
Crabtree, P. 3	3	0	1	3	2	0
Wigdor 1	1	1	1	0	0	0
Totals 33	33	2	6	24	5	5

Snelling.

	AB	R	H	PO	A	E
Brown, 3b	4	1	2	0	1	1
Tew, C.	3	0	1	14	2	0
Porter, C.F.	3	0	0	0	0	0
Anderson, S.S.	4	0	0	0	3	0
Schults, 1b	4	1	1	10	1	0
McCann, R.F.	3	0	0	0	0	0
Bird, L.F.	4	0	1	1	0	0
Vaugh, 2b	4	0	1	1	1	1
Lushen, P.	4	1	1	1	3	0
Totals	33	3	7	27	11	2

Summary—Two base hits: Kawa, Brown. Stolen bases: Houck, Kawa, Guiger and Truso. Hit by pitcher: by Crabtree 1 (McCann), by Lushen 1 (Guiger). Struck out by Crabtree 5, by Lushen 14. Base on balls: off Crabtree 2, off Lushen 3. Earned runs: Grant 1, Snelling 0.

GRANT VS. FT. DES MOINES

June 18, 1919.

Greatly fatigued after a 20 mile ride in an army "bus" and following the previous two strenuous games, the team arrived at Des Moines and without a minute's rest, donned their uniforms and engaged the local team. It is not much to the discredit of the team that they lost 12-0, for before the team could get their bearings in the first inning 7 runs were scored by Des Moines as the result of 7 errors by Grant. The team was completely demoralized and away off their mettle, in fact hardly recognizable as being the Camp Grant team in the previous games, as the 13 errors on their part would testify.

The defeat was all the harder to swallow, for the Camp Dodge team, which we had beaten the day before, had recently defeated the Des Moines team by an overwhelming score.

Sgt. Frank Hoar is by way of earning a reputation as a steeple-jack. This is the second time he has "shinned" to the top of our flag-pole to get down the Flag when the rope broke.

Hosp. Sgt. VorKeller must have believed the old saying that "music is elevating" when he took his position in a ditch, at the Decoration Day flagraising. The trouble was, there was no music to elevate him, for even his trusty warriors can't tell when to start when they can't see the director.

(Continued from page 3)

growth of military bands, however, from these two nuclei and as the years passed they were developed until the present stage of perfection.

The French and Germans seem to have perfected the art of military music and were the first to actually have a band attached to each separate regiment.

Frederick the Great of Prussia had all his bands massed from time to time, this being the first use of military bands in this way.

The inspiration of martial music is an undoubted fact, and no army would be complete without its Regimental Bands. A parade of soldiers without a band is a tame affair, and how interesting it is with the band to troop the line and lead the march past in review.

There is no more inspiring sight in the world than to see a regiment of infantry troop the colors; with the band playing and the rifles sparkling, and the colors snapping in the breeze. And when the day is over when retreat sounds, and the band plays the National Anthem, while the flag is lowered, what could be more stirring.

When the band gives its concert after Guard Mounting everyone gathers around to hear. Then when the semi-weekly concert is given, how it is enjoyed. What is better than to sit in the cool evening air and listen to a good military band rendering good music?

There have been many famous bands developed from the primitive organizations previously mentioned. The Guards Bands of England and Belgium, the Band of the Guarde Republique of France; our own Marine Band, than which none can excel, but one, to us, and that is our own band, an organization of which we have just rights to be proud. From its inception in April, 1918, it became a success. The men who composed it were all good musicians and took pride in their work. They have just reason to be so for in the year and more of the existence of the band there has not been one case of absence without leave or a reason for reprimand. Under the able direction of Hosp. Sgt. Henry P. Vorkeller, M.D., the band reached this state of perfection which made it the best organization in this neighborhood. It is a matter of record that they were the best band in Chicago during the third Liberty Loan drive, and the fact that they have been called upon to participate in the Fourth and Fifth drives is an evidence of their capability. We sadly missed them when they were away and welcomed their return.

It will be with deep regret that we will witness the disintegration of our

band in July when the members w
be discharged. The unfailing goc
will with which they performed the
duties and the excellent manner
their performance will always be r
membered with pleasure. We have e
joyed the concerts given, and our fe
would not keep still when they playe
for the dances. May each member r
turn to civil life with the knowledge
our good wishes and may they all me
with the success which merit demand

Charles S. Elliot.
Captain, Sanitary Corps, U. S.
Adjutant.

THE COTILLION DANCE

The Cotillion Dance held at the Cor
valescent House on Thursday evenin
was undoubtedly one of the most er
joyable entertainments given the er
listed men of the Detachment durin
the past season.

The Convalescent House had bee
very tastily decorated for the occasio
and presented an inviting appearance
The ladies arrived at about eigh
o'clock and a grand march precede
the dance program.   At nine o'cloc
the Cotillion commenced under th
able guidance of a director from Ch
cago. A number of very novel feature
were introduced greatly adding to th
amusement, and the Cotillion whic
lasted about an hour and a half prove
a huge success judging by the er
thusiasm displayed by the participant
Perhaps at no previous dance given a
the Red Cross House has such a con
genial spirit pervaded, as was show
at this dance.

A great deal of credit is due to in
dividuals and committees who b
their untiring efforts made this ver
successful party possible. In this con
nection very favorable mention shoul
be made of the creditable manner i
which Vorkeller's Orchestra per
formed.

(Continued from page 7)

Still wet from the press, Pvt. Wi
liard B. Prather's "Hand-Book of Mi
Information," a compendium of a
most-facts well worth a place in any
one's attic.   A careful study of thi
book will give you a fund of near
knowledge that should put you acros
in any conversation. A big value fc
the money if only for the smoothnes
of its "line." For sale at all hardwar
stores at twenty-nine cents and wa
tax.

Rockford's welcome on June 10tl
to its returned heroes in Companies I
and K of the 129th Inf., 33rd Div.,
course, called for the services of tl
band. A nice warm parade of a mi
and a quarter, under a blazing sun an
a buzzing aeroplane was "enjoyed"
after which the assembled congreg
tion sojourned with us to Blackhaw

Park, where we took turns with the enviable Barber-Coleman band at furnishing music for the boys while they demolished a perfectly good barbecued dinner. A little later, we took a hand (or in fact, two of them) in the wrecking game, to the entire demoralization of the cooking staff. After dinner, the two bands took turns at playing and talking to the pretty girls. Of course, our boys were better at the former. Was it hot on that hill? I'll say it was. The return to camp was made just in time for retreat.

Our otherwise genial friends, Stiverson and Riha, had an opportunity to demonstrate the spirit of the "Fighting Base" recently, when the M. P.'s took a fancy to and appropriated to their own use our faithful mascot, "Spot." Needless to say, "Spot" still responds to the band roll-call.

All that worries us is: Who's going to keep "O" in business after the band goes home?

While parading in Chicago, on the Victory Loan Drive, we met our old friend, Major Baum (looking fine in "civies"). We were more than pleased to hear that the Major has been promoted to the rank of Lieutenant Colonel in the Medical Reserve Corps. The smokes were excellent.

The "Misplaced Eye-brow Brigade" remains constant. Having lost Corp. John Stucki, who slipped one over on his with a razor, we have gained Pvt. Ross Stiverson, who has acquired a neatly sculptored black one that is a joy to every one of his girls.

Corp. Ott's latest capture is a widow with two beautiful children. You're doing better, Corporal.

"Spot" has gotten so fastidious since joining the band that he will eat only the choicest bits (such as they are) that the mess-hall can furnish, and when there is any choice, always selects a Hospital Sergeant's bed on which to sleep.

(Continued from page 13)
The members of the band wish, at this time of parting, to express to the Enlisted Men, Officers, Nurses, Student Nurses, Red Cross, K. C. and Y. M. C. A. workers and to Lieut. Col. H. C. Michie, our Commanding Officer, our appreciation of the many kindnesses shown us during our stay here, and of the whole-hearted support and co-operation afforded us by the entire personnel of the Base Hospital.

Some time since, our friend Jim Bennett, desiring to write a letter to one of his many admirers, but lacking the necessary "makings," hollered from his bunk for some stationery. Quick as a flash, our witty drummer, Bodenschatz, came back with: "Why don't you raise your window and make your own station airy?"

In the morning, these nice summery days, we bless the farmer who so kindly planted the two fruitful cherry trees beside our barracks, but by noon, there is nearly always someone who would like to meet the aforesaid farmer in a dark alley.

Can someone explain why "Spot," when looking for a scrap, always hunts out an officer's dog? Ft. Leavenworth for you, "Spot," if you don't watch out!

The band boys won't have to depend on word of mouth to convey impressions of their life in the army to their grand-children, if one may judge by the number of albums being filled with snap-shots.

It may have been hot work, but the boys have felt they were doing something worth while when they have stood out in the sun and played short concerts for the patients, lately.

It looked almost like a "free for all," for a minute, the other day, when a conductor on the C., M. & St. P. tried to use rough tactics on our faithful mascot. "Spot," who had been unthinkingly taken into one of the coaches on the way to Genoa, Ill., where we played for the home-coming.

The auto ride from Genoa, that night, sure prepared the boys for some strenuous "bunk fatigue."

(Continued from Page 11)
to be furnished them to get back to their civilian occupations, and we hope that each will go back a bigger and better man for the fellowship he has enjoyed in the months the band has been in service.

THE BASE HOSPITAL BAND

July the sixth comes on apace;
We hope they'll add no days of grace.
Our time is up; our work is done;
We did our best; the war is won.

For o'er a year our place we've filled,
Though not a German have we killed;
And though we've never fired a gun,
We've done our bit to beat the Hun.

Some had to go—some had to stay;
Time never came they set the day
For us to go across the sea
To cheer our boys in Germany.

We had no chance at "over there,"
But in our place, we've done our share
To cheer the folks who had to stay
And run the Base in the proper way.

When cash was needed, the war to win,
We tightened our belts and buckled in
On the Liberty Loan and worked like Hell
And Chicago's quota helped to sell.

The Red Cross drive and the call to share
In the War Activities found us there,
From morning to night, in the midst of the fray,
Bringing in dollars till they'd won the day.

In the Victory Loan, the drive we led,
Toward paying our debt to the boys who bled.
We toured the state on a special train
And did our best, in sun or rain.

We found many towns all ready to stop,
But we stirred them up—put them over the top;
Met mighty hard work,. but waded right in,
And with that sort of spirit, just couldn't help win.

That's the spirit we've tried to put in our work
Here in camp or on tour, and never to shirk.
Our days at the Base will soon be past,
But the friendships we've made will endure to the last.

Pvt. 1st/Cl, H. R. Sweet.

Everything in
Military Clothing

UNIFORMS—Serge, O. D., Whipcord, Gabardine, Khaki..........$10 to $35

BREECHES—Whipcord, Bedford Cord, Serge, O. D., Khaki.....$4.95 to $12.50

SHOES—Large selection, among which is the Munson Last Army Shoe, specially priced at......................$5.50

BOOTS—Cordovan, Trench Lace, Moccasin Trench Boots.................$15

PUTTEES—Cowhide, Pigskin, Cordovan....................$2.50 to $7.50

Rubbers, Overshoes, Hip Boots, Hose, Kapo Coats.

BAGS AND SUITCASES—Big lot of various styles..................$1 up

RAINCOATS—Many with detachable lining.....................$15 to $35

KNOX HATS—A famous hat, special at $5

CAPS—Overseas caps, many silk-lined, $1 and $2

CHEVRONS—Domestic and imported gold and silver..............5c and 15c

Underwear, Handerkerchiefs, Belts, Vests, Gloves, Sweaters.

GOODS—Our merchandise is unbeatable, for we have a skilled buyer who knows the market and is able to purchase large lots at sharply reduced prices.

PRICES—Here is where you benefit, because we pass on to you the saving gained by this expert, country-wide buying.

SERVICE—We have a number of trained and quick salesmen, who understand the stock and like to satisfy you. We have an alteration and tailor service that is unequalled. We are open evenings and Sunday.

LOCATION—At your very door. Just follow Service Street north—known as Base Hospital Road to the Camp entrance.

The Harry Hamill Company

Kishwaukee---Camp Entrance---Zone 1

"At the Foot of the Hill"